There's a lot of things in life that I know nothing about. But one thing I know for sure is this: life gives us a lot of gifts. Some of them come wrapped up in the ugliest wrapping paper ever. These gifts are extra special. You have to un-wrap them, layer by layer, knowing that what's inside is incredible.

My name is Jackie Sabuda. I am a cancer survivor. I wake up every day counting my blessings. I wake up every day looking forward to the next adventure. Sometimes, things don't work out exactly as I had hoped or planned. But when I take the time to think about it, sometimes different outcomes are even better!

My mom calls me the Queen of Mind over Matter. Mind over Matter – everyone's heard that before, right? It's deciding you're going to get through something really hard in life, no matter what. It's never, ever, ever giving up, no matter what. It's actually "thinking" yourself well again, making yourself stronger and healthier with your own thoughts. Dance is a BIG part of that for me. It's like therapy –

Dance Therapy! When you're dancing, you're not thinking about being sick. When you're dancing, you're not thinking about the bad day you had. Actually after you dance, and you think back about your day, you realize it wasn't so bad after all.

This book is a collection of some of my favorite dance quotes and some of my favorite dance pictures. I believe that all dancers all over the world are connected somehow. I think after you read some of the quotes in this book, you'll feel the same way – we ARE connected through the art and love of dance!

Jackie Sabuda

"The body says what words cannot." (Martha Graham)

"Hold fast to dreams, for if dreams die, life is a broken

winged bird that cannot fly."
(Lanston Hughes)

"Dancing is the poetry of the foot." (John Dryden)

"Never miss a chance to dance."

"Find a place inside where there's joy and the joy will burn out the pain." (Joseph Campbell)

"You don't have to be great to start, but you have to start to be great." (Zig Ziglar)

"Don't wait for the perfect moment. Take the moment and make it perfect."

"Happiness does not come from doing easy work but from the afterglow of satisfaction that comes after the achievement of a difficult task that demanded our best." (Theodore Isaac Rubin)

"You will never know your limits unless you push yourself to them."

"I really reject that kind of comparison that says, Oh, he is the best. This is the second best. There is no such thing." (Mikhail Baryshnikov)

"Dancing is my obsession. My life." (Mikhail Baryshnikov)

"When you dance, your purpose is not to get to a certain place on the floor. It's to enjoy each step along the way." (Wayne Dyer)

"Practice means to perform, over and over again in the face of all obstacles, some act of vision, of faith, of desire. Practice is a means of inviting the perfection desired." (Martha Graham)

"No matter how many times I break down, there is always a little piece of me that says, NO, you're not done yet, GET BACK UP!"

"I don't remember not dancing. When I realized I was alive and these were my parents, and I could walk and talk, I could dance." (Gregory Hines)

"I love tap dancing. I love my tap shoes. I get so inspired, so filled up. It's like I need a shot of whiskey, and I don't even drink." (Gregory Hines)

"The one thing that you have that nobody else has is you. Your voice, your mind, your story, your vision. So write and draw, and

build and play and dance and live as only you can." (Neil Gaiman)

"The higher up you go, the more mistakes you are allowed. Right at the top, if you make enough of them, it's considered to be your style." (Fred Astaire)

"We all thought we were trying to create some kind of magic or joy, and you know, that's what you do up there. You dance love, you dance joy, and you dance dreams." (Gene Kelly)

"You know you're a dancer when you practice a routine in your head at all times."

"To dance is to be out of yourself. Larger, more beautiful, more powerful." (Agnes de Mille)

"When you feel sad, DANCE!" (Gene Kelly)

"I don't have to be on the dance floor at the studio. The WHOLE WORLD is my dance floor!" (Jackie Sabuda)

Jackie Sabuda

"We dance for laughter, we dance for tears. We dance for madness, we dance for fears. We dance for hopes, we dance for screams. We are the dancers; we create the dreams."

"Dance is bigger than the physical body. When you extend your arm, it doesn't stop at the end of your fingers, because you're dancing bigger than that; you're dancing spirit." (Judith Jamison)

"Dancing is the way to Heaven."

"Life isn't about waiting for the storm to pass. It's about learning to dance in the rain."

"I have chosen to be HAPPY because it's good for my health." (Voltaire)

"Dancers are instruments, like a piano the choreographer plays." (George Balanchine)

"Dancing is like dreaming with your feet!" (Constanze)

"If I could tell you what it meant, there would be no point in dancing it." (Isadora Duncan)

"To touch, to move, to inspire. This is the true gift of dance." *(Aubrey Lynch)*

"The creative process is not controlled by a switch you can simply turn on or off; it's with you all the time." *(Alvin Ailey)*

"No artist is ahead of his time. He is time; the others are just behind the times." (Martha Graham)

"The truest expression of a people is in its dance and in its music. Bodies never lie." (Agnes de Mille)

"If anything at all, perfection is finally attained not when there is no longer anything to add but when there is no longer anything to take away." (Maria Tallchief)

"Master technique and then forget about it and be natural."
(Anna Pavlova)

"If I cannot dance, I shall die!"
(Anna Pavlova)

"There is a bit of insanity in dancing that does everybody a great deal of good." (Edwin Denby)

"I want to see the movement, not the effort behind it." (from the movie "Center Stage")

"Life begins at the end of your comfort zone." (Neale Donald Walsch)

"Dance for yourself. If someone understands, good. If not, then no matter; go right on doing what you love." (Lois Hurst)

"I do not try to dance better than anyone else. I only try to dance better than myself." (Mikhail Baryshnikov)

"To watch us dance is to hear our hearts speak." (Hopi Indian saying)

"Dance every performance as if it were your last." (Erik Bruhn)

"Today you are YOU; that is TRUER than true. There is NO ONE alive who is YOUER than YOU!" (Dr. Seuss)

"Kids: they dance before they learn there is anything that isn't music." (William Stafford)

Jackie Sabuda – The Cat (7 years old)

"There are short-cuts to happiness, and dancing is one of them." (Vicki Baum)

"People dance because dance can change things. One move, can make you believe like there's

something more. One move, can set a whole generation free."
(from the movie, "Step Up 3-D")

"Any problem in the world can be solved by dancing." (James Brown)

"Dance expresses joy better than anything else." (Bob Fosse)

"The essence of all art is to have pleasure in giving pleasure." (Mikhail Baryshnikov)

Jackie Sabuda – Golden Glow (10 years old)

"In life as in dance, grace glides on blistered feet." (Alice Abrams)

Jackie Sabuda – Rodeo (11 years old)

"It is of course, possible to dance a prayer." (Glade Byron Addams)

"It's just about following your heart. If there's something you want to do, don't let anything get in your way." (Dawnell Dryja)

"You can't make a pointe if you don't understand the details."

Jackie Sabuda – Golden Glow (10 years old)

"Kids that think ballet class is boring, but want to be great dancers – I'll never understand that. It's like wanting to read without learning the alphabet!"
(Jackie Sabuda)

Jackie Sabuda

"Different styles of dance are like vitamins. Dance vitamins! Vitamin Ballet=helps you stay balanced and centered (very important vitamin! Everyone should take Vitamin Ballet!) Vitamin Tap=serious stress reliever and great for your heart! (Forget your troubles with Vitamin Tap!) Vitamin Acro=very

important for strength and flexibility (try Vitamin Acro – you'll love it!) Vitamins Jazz, Lyrical, Modern & Contemporary=excellent vitamins for your heart and soul (take these vitamins and you'll feel better instantly!) Vitamin Hip Hop=helps you to express yourself and BE yourself (take Vitamin Hip Hop and you'll feel more alive!) Musical Theatre vitamins=the vitamins that taste like candy! (Musical Theatre vitamins are so much fun, you don't even realize how good they are for you!) Hawaiian, African, Indian, Folk Dancing and every other kind of dancing vitamins=are ALL good for you! Try them, you'll like them! Pointe vitamins=a stronger form of Vitamin Ballet (take Pointe vitamins only when you're ready. Warning: once you start taking Pointe vitamins, you'll never want to stop!)" (from Jackie Sabuda's "Why Dance?" report)

If you want to be a great dancer, you have to study great dancers. I've been lucky enough to work with some fantastic dancers and choreographers. And the ones I haven't had a chance to work with (yet!) I've studied. Some dancers and choreographers, I'll never know – they're dancing on the clouds in

Heaven above. But they left their lessons on film. So I watch – over and over again. And learn. George Balanchine, Bob Fosse, Gene Kelly, Fred Astaire, Ann Miller, Maria Tallchief, Anna Pavlova ...the list is endless!

Even the dancers who are dancing on the clouds in Heaven – we're ALL connected through the art and love of dance!

Thank you for sharing your love of dance with me!

Jackie Sabuda
Author, Dancer

Made in the USA
Charleston, SC
16 April 2014